PAUSE,

SHIFT

and

Refresh

Seven Arts of Establishing
Harmonious Oneness

Ericka Brian

BALBOA.
PRESS

A DIVISION OF HAY HOUSE

All scripture quotations are from the The Holy Bible. Ed. Church of Jesus Christ of Latter-day Saints. Salt Lake City: Church of Jesus Christ of Latter-day Saints, 2013. Web. Authorized King James Vers. © 2013 by Intellectual Reserve, Inc. All rights reserved.

Balboa Press books may be ordered through booksellers or by contacting:

Balboa Press
A Division of Hay House
1663 Liberty Drive
Bloomington, IN 47403
www.balboapress.com
1 (877) 407-4847

Because of the dynamic nature of the Internet, any web addresses or links contained in this book may have changed since publication and may no longer be valid. The views expressed in this work are solely those of the author and do not necessarily reflect the views of the publisher, and the publisher hereby disclaims any responsibility for them.

The author of this book does not dispense medical advice or prescribe the use of any technique as a form of treatment for physical, emotional, or medical problems without the advice of a physician, either directly or indirectly. The intent of the author is only to offer information of a general nature to help you in your quest for emotional and spiritual well-being. In the event you use any of the information in this book for yourself, which is your constitutional right, the author and the publisher assume no responsibility for your actions.

Any people depicted in stock imagery provided by Thinkstock are models, and such images are being used for illustrative purposes only.
Certain stock imagery © Thinkstock.

Print information available on the last page.

ISBN: 978-1-5043-8496-4 (sc)
ISBN: 978-1-5043-8498-8 (hc)
ISBN: 978-1-5043-8497-1 (e)

Library of Congress Control Number: 2017911998

Balboa Press rev. date: 08/16/2017

Your level of peace is directly related to the level of intimacy you have with your inner companion.

—Unknown

Contents

Acknowledgments:
Meet the Muses

To my grandparents, thank you for your faith in a better future and for your unconditional love. Thank you for teaching me how to persevere despite the challenges in life, to lead with a compassionate heart, and to be faithful when facing adversity.

To Grandma Judy and Grandpa Robert Carsten, thank you for being beautiful examples of God-fearing spirits. The level of commitment you have embraced in caring for your family is inspiring.

To the Brian family, thank you for being examples of faith, unconditional love, and the gift of prayer.

To my uncle Manny, thank you for being my role model. Your love, compassion and dedication have greatly contributed to the family and society.

To my parents, who taught me to strive for excellence

and to be resourceful even in the most undesirable experiences, thank you.

To my aunts and uncles, thank you for your love and support—especially you, Punky, Nina, Aunty Maria, and Aunty Lorraine.

To my sisters, Evelyn and Emily, thank you for your sisterly love through the years and for being my first audience.

To my children, who have taught me the greatest love, joy, and growth of all, thank you.

To Zack Richards, thank you for your love, support and for enriching my life. May we continue to grow and explore this beautiful journey, inspiring generations to come.

To my friends Chelsea Freund, Rommy Pinney, Emmanuel Soriano, Delores Davis, Stacy Smith, Cynthia Despain, Dee Ann Almeter and Barbara Guy, thank you for being examples of courage and support.

To my stroke survivor friends and their caregivers, thank you for showing me great examples of love, strength, humor, perseverance, and courage.

Lastly, but just as importantly, to my future friends, clients, and teachers, thank you. May we all embrace the gifts within, lead with the spirit, and love one another.

Introduction: The Journey

Pause, Shift, and Refresh came to me as I was helping a coworker submit her PTO (paid time off) request. I found myself repeating, "Pause, press shift, and wait for the computer to refresh." *Pause, shift, and refresh.* Once I became aware of the words leaving my mouth, I awakened. At that moment, my verbal expression was feeding a part of my soul that I had neglected. I had been seeking guidance along my journey, but who knew that I would find clarity when I was not intentionally seeking it? What if our answers are truly found in the act of service to others?

As the founder of Return to Yourself Wellness, I am a huge advocate of enhancing quality of life by nourishing the body, mind, and spirit. My motivation— to pause, shift, and refresh—is derived from nature, my body, and the universe.

My spiritual journey began when I was eighteen. I enrolled in a yoga class at Crafton Hills College in Yucaipa, California, not having a clue what I was getting myself in to. On the first day of class I was kindly welcomed by the yoga instructor, who was seriously the hottest man I had ever seen. Now, I don't know if it was his yogic energy radiating or his shoulder-length hair and strong arms, but whatever it was I wanted to learn more about this man and why out of all possibilities in the world, he wanted to teach yoga.

I was the student who lacked flexibility, coordination, and focus. When the instructor encouraged us to lift our right legs, my reflex was to lift my left leg. I was so unaware of my body and its reactions that I was just moving in a knee-jerk fashion. After learning so much during this amazing semester, I moved to Arizona to pursue a relationship with a man I had met online. Now, my conditional mind would tell you that this was a big mistake, but my spirit believes there are no mistakes. Regardless, this move changed my life.

You may be asking yourself, "What is the conditional mind?" I will refer to this concept often. The conditional mind is a state of mind cultivated by the perceptions of past experiences and the things you have been taught. The people who reared you and the educational system within which you were raised influence the conditional mind. Most likely you may have taken on many attributes, characteristics, habits, and behaviors that were passed down to you from previous generations. Therefore, many of your behaviors and decisions have been consciously or unconsciously passed down to you. As you read this book, I highly encourage you to evaluate your conditional mind. Write down any questions, judgments, thoughts, or ideas.

My yogic experience expands deeper into my childhood, my education, and the decisions made in my early twenties; however, we'll save that for my next book, *Emerging from the Shadow*.

Before moving to Arizona, my best friend, Emmanuel Soriano, knowing I had taken up yoga, gave me a book he thought I would enjoy. It was *The Seven Spiritual Laws of Success* by Dr. Deepak Chopra. At the time, the book did not resonate with me, but I held on to it. Thank the heavens I did, because when I turned twenty-five I stumbled across it during a time of sincere desperation. I had hit rock bottom in my life. My relationships were falling apart, I was losing someone who I cared dearly about to alcoholism, and I had lost my spark for living. I had completely disengaged from life and was focused only on working, finishing school, performing motherly duties, and being a responsible wife. I made no time for myself; nor did I become aware of intentionally desiring to live a life. I was on autopilot, stuck on *do and repeat*.

Once I stumbled across the book and began rereading it, there was an instant connection. The words resonated within my soul. I was hungry to know more and wanted to know who this Dr. Deepak Chopra was. For all I knew, this could have been a one-book wonder for him. However, after some research, I discovered I was wrong. This man had written over sixty books that had been translated into many different languages, and he operated a center in San Diego. I was compelled to go to one of his retreats, but they were all too expensive. At this point in my life, my children and I were living paycheck to paycheck. I knew if there was a will there was a way, but I was already working two jobs, seven days a week. I had never taken a day off from work because I was afraid to ask. I began praying about my situation. Prayer was not a common practice at this stage of my life. Previously, I had only prayed when I was with my grandmothers. After praying consistently, I felt a great sense of peace and believed somehow all would be well.

My birthday was approaching as I was contemplating how I was going to afford to attend one of Dr. Chopra's retreats. One day, after my inspirational ceremony of studying the Chopra Center pictures and envisioning myself there, my mother called me to inquire about my birthday. Jokingly, I said, "Mom, I know what you are getting me for my birthday." She was amused and questioned what it could be. I told her of my interest in the retreat, and she said yes. Two weeks later, I stepped foot on the grounds at La Costa. It was one of the most beautiful places I had ever been. Shortly thereafter, a tingling sensation moved throughout my body, suggesting something amazing was about to embrace me, something transformational. As these overwhelming, tantalizing sensations took over and encouraged me, I took a deep breath, and suddenly the spark of life came back: I felt alive!

The "Weekend Within" retreat was absolutely amazing. Getting to meet Dr. Chopra, who previously I didn't even know existed, was life changing. I felt as though this man and I shared the same heart of compassion, the compelling drive to inspire and live the best quality of life possible. All of this was in me, despite the hurtful and hopeless foundations I had emerged from; I was determined to return to the center. My life changed dramatically. I began to practice the law of intention and desire to help me return to the center. Suddenly, I had more opportunities to earn additional income, and I began to save money. I used the extra income to purchase a weeklong retreat called "Seduction of Spirit" and was encouraged to complete another called "Journey into Healing," after which I successfully applied for the teacher's path at Chopra Center University. I embraced this invitation of the universe and persevered.

Throughout this important and timely journey, I graduated from Chopra University, earned my bachelor's degree from Arizona State University, became a nutritional therapist via Health Science Academy, and became a Latter-day Saint. I became a more aware parent, got a divorce, became a single mom, managed two to four jobs at a time, purchased my first house, and founded my own business. People asked "How did you do it"? My response, "Through constant and sincere prayer and by not allowing myself the option to do otherwise." Choices are offered by the many influences in our lives as well as our intentions. Choose your environment wisely, for it will become your external body, which will influence your internal body (state of awareness). The state of your internal body will highly influence your present moment.

During this journey, I quickly learned that I had been living in a state of fear that had been simmering in the toxicity of my insecurities, doubts, and despair. When I connected with the infinite possibility of my intentions and started being led by my heart and passions, I became unstoppable.

My darling, when you avoid the deepest desires of your heart for any reason, those desires will begin to dim. Just like a muscle in your body, if you don't use it, it will weaken. If there is anything beneficial you get out of this book, I hope it is that you will own your light and live the life you desire. Pause and observe the life you are living. Ask: Is this life what you ultimately desire? Are you stressed within your comfort level? Are you evolving? Are your relationships nourishing? Learn how to shift into intentional thoughts and actions. Live your life with purpose and gratitude. Refresh into your life with a new perspective and drive to accomplish your dreams. Establish the art of harmonious oneness, as I did, by returning to yourself.

There are seven chapters in this book that hold the secrets, techniques, and tips by which I established harmonious oneness during the most transformational years of my life. Grab a pen and journal during this reading experience. Honor things, ideas, images, and sensations that surface by writing them down. Before reading each chapter, I encourage you to pray. Even if you have never prayed before, close your eyes, sit in a comfortable position, or kneel. Speak aloud or silently your desires or intent to learn what it is you read. As for your heart, be open, giving yourself the opportunity to heal and release what no longer is serving you. Jot down any intentions you desire. After your reading session, allow yourself time to meditate. Sit in silence and reflect on how you are translating the context, ideas, images, or sensations that surfaced. Document your experience and enjoy.

With the help of this book, I hope you enhance your awareness to pause, shift, and refresh into the state you were once in, before being influenced by your world.

 # The Art of You

"*Deep within us, there is something profoundly known, not consciously, but subconsciously; a quiet truth, that is not a version of something, but an original knowing. What this absolute truth [identity] is may be none of our business ... but it is there, guiding us along the path of greater becoming; a true awareness. It is so self-sustaining that our recognition of it is not required. We are offspring of such a powerfully divine force – Creator of all things known and unknown.*"

—T.F. Hodge, *From Within I Rise: Spiritual Triumph Over Death and Conscious Encounters with "The Divine Presence"*

You hold the strength of the mountains and the tranquility of the sea. As you explore the art of *you*, I encourage you to release any perceptions that you've cultivated of yourself. Your perceptions of yourself have heavily influenced your experiences through your thoughts and choices. Give yourself permission to dive into the art of you. Find the foundation in your value and purpose as you shift into your higher self.

"Higher self" is an expression that I will use to describe *you* in the purest form of yourself—the one who leads with an open heart and a kind mind; the one who is aware of the influences of the emotional mind or the world yet mindfully chooses to live a life full of intention and purpose.

Finding your value can be simple. You are a child of a creator. Whether you want to limit your existence to the physical senses of this world or beyond into the spiritual realm, you have been created to exist in your own creative way. You have unique talents, abilities, and passions that no one else has. It is your responsibility, as an awake being, to share your unique talents, abilities, and passions. There are things in this world that only you will be able to do. Nature, including the people of this world, has waited for your arrival. Yes, you are that magnificent! Therefore, don't waste your life energy on distractions that keep you from expressing your unique gifts or manipulate your physical form hoping to be noticed. Know that in this moment, you are enough. The world is awaiting for you to shine your light.

Some known distractions that might be in your way: watching pornography, overindulging in physical objects, accumulating without giving, holding on to experiences, and/or being dishonest.

Following the Ten Commandments and the eight limbs of yoga by Patanjali has guided me to shift into a higher state of myself and to explore my value and purpose according to the wisdom of the commandments and limbs. Each person is precious in the eyes of his or her conscious creator, so we have been given the tools and guidance to live lives full of value and purpose. I understand that there are many people who struggle with the concept of believing in a God or creator. Give yourself permission to release any ideals you have developed over the years and take time to reflect on each commandment and limb. When you can release ideals you have developed, you give yourself space to reflect. Then ask yourself these questions: What does this mean to me? Can I see myself benefiting from this commandment or limb?

Below I will list the commandments and eight limbs of yoga giving you *my reflection* on each one.

The Ten Commandments

As a Mormon, I use the version of the Ten Commandments found on www.LDS.org, which is a great resource for finding doctrines, spiritual talks, and music to fill your soul.

1. "Thou shalt have no other Gods before me"

In church, we are told that our God is a jealous God and that we must only praise him. That didn't resonate too well with me. Therefore, I began to explore this understanding and what it meant for me. I learned that by believing in multiple gods, I was becoming spiritually exhausted. I was praising all that I had come to know, yet I felt the need to continue to seek because something within was not complete. I found myself in spiritual discontentment and formed an unstable foundation. With an unstable foundation, I was more likely to cave to temptations that would lead me away from the purest form of myself.

2. "Thou shalt not make unto thee any graven image"

When making graven images, we become distracted by what has been created. For example, we may be distracted by the sex or the perceived nationality of the image created. We should look within through prayer in order to connect with the source of all that is.

3. "Thou shalt not take the name of the lord thy God in vain"

It's important we never take any name in vain or use harming or derogatory language. When I've used a derogatory expression, it has felt empty or fueled with negative emotion. We have the responsibility, as conscious beings, to respect all that is for what it is. Use your precious words wisely. May your words and expressions be fueled with love, compassion, and understanding.

4. "Remember the Sabbath Day, to keep it holy"

Taking one day out of the week to intentionally be spiritual has been a blessing. I was once working seven days a week. I had very little time to fill my spiritual cup, which was compromising my foundations; I found myself weak when I came face-to-face with temptation. Taking the day off from work to practice my faith and be with my family has given me a beautiful perspective on life. I choose to slow down and enjoy time with my family. I do my best to try to infuse the understanding of Sabbath to all the days of the week, encouraging me to slow down and be in the light of my heavenly Father.

5. "Honor thy father and mother"

Honoring those who gave us life gives us the gift of humility. There were times I didn't agree with my parents or the choices they made. My grandmother would tell me, "Love them anyway." *"Love them anyway"* were words I lived by for all encounters. See if you can forgive and love those closest to you; then you can forgive and love those who come and go.

6. "Thou shalt not kill"

For obvious reasons, we don't ever want to cause anyone pain or death, no matter what they have done to us.

7. Thou shalt not commit adultery.

Oh adultery, a pain that can last a lifetime once inflicted. I know this pain all too well and would not wish it on the meanest person I know. I really don't see the point in engaging in such acts. What I do know is a person who does commit adultery is feeling desperate. One significant other shared that the reason why he cheated two times was because he needed validation that he was attractive. The third time was because he fell in love, but that love, unfortunately, only lasted two weeks. As much as I wished to help him with my words and body, I knew that the level of sadness and desperation lingering in his soul was not of my doing. This was bigger than me, bigger than our relationship.

In every relationship, we have the responsibility to verbalize what our needs are. If we don't, we will become desperate. Unfortunately, desperation has led to plenty of unnecessary suffering. Love and respect yourself enough to speak your needs, for you do deserve what you desire. Love those who choose to be in your life, for they too deserve what they desire.

8. "Thou shalt not steal"

We should never take anything that is not our own without permission. The feelings of guilt, shame, and dishonesty will be overwhelming; never allowing us to truly enjoy what is now in our possession.

9. "Thou shalt not bear false witness"

As a child, to cope with the pain of my life events, I would begin to fantasize about living a different life with different people around me who couldn't hurt me. I've come to know the blessing and the curse that goes along with this coping mechanism; the blessing is that you create a happy place emotionally, but the curse is that you will never truly learn from your experiences if you are not completely attentive, which means the experiences will continue to repeat themselves until their value is learned. Also, the more we fantasize, the more illusions we create. I noticed that I would try to replicate people I loved who hurt me by attracting other similar people to me, hoping they would treat me better. However, I only created an unrealistic expectation they would never meet.

10. "Thou shalt not covet"

In our society, it's very easy to think there's no need to get married. In fact, getting married a second time didn't even make financial sense to me. I had much more investments than my significant other did. Why would I jeopardize all that I had created for my two kids and me for another relationship? A relationship can fail, after all.

Here is what I know: Being married has blessed the lives of many that I know. Being married decreases the temptation of risky or promiscuous behavior, which would decrease sexual transmitted disease and unwanted pregnancies. Also, there is something sacred about having a life partner. Working in a hospital setting for many years, I've witnessed some patients with spouses and others without. I can say that watching couples hold their love ones' hand during their last days is heart breaking but comforting to know the sacrifice and love shared over the years.

I found being in a relationship and not being married

it's easy to give up and not continue to work through the turbulent times. It's also easier to become easily persuaded by others. There were a few men who dated many women prior to meeting me, and it was easy for them to jump into something more convenient. By following this commandment, I have spared myself unnecessary heartache, faced my demons, and found a deeper level of love.

Eight Limbs of Yoga

Now let's look at the eight limbs of yoga by Patanjali.

1. Yama—ethical standards.

   a. Ahimsa—practicing non-violence.
      Ahimsa relates to commandment number six, "Thou shalt not kill." What I love about this ethical standard is that like the commandment, we may not kill. However, partaking in a violent act, whether through words or actions, is easier to do and is also forbidden.

   b. Satya—speaking truthfully.
      Satya relates to commandment nine, "Thou

shalt not bear false witness." Do your best to be truthful. If you can't in the moment, then perhaps you should embrace silence.

c. Brahmacharya—exercising appropriate sexual control.

In today's world, it's very easy to indulge in sexual deeds. Sex is exploited, and somehow that makes a lack of sexual control acceptable. However, not being in control of sexual desires can lead to getting a sexually transmitted disease or having an unwanted pregnancy. There is a different level of intimacy when you wait until you truly know someone before you give yourself completely. I highly recommend you wait until marriage.

d. Asteya—being honest.

When dishonesty is embraced, its residue will linger in your mind. You have the choice to travel light, without carrying any residue from your actions or the actions of others. Chose to be honest and travel light.

e. Aparigraha—generosity.

In the Bible, we are taught to give 10 percent of our earnings to the church. It's our way to tithe. However, our generosity should not stop there. In every experience, there is an opportunity to expend our unique talents and skills. Show the world your gifts, talents and skill sets. It can be as simple as sharing your beautiful smile or donating money. Whatever it may be, just do it.

2. Niyama—spiritual standards.

a. Saucha—purity.

Travel as the purest form of yourself. Before doing so, partake in acts that contribute to your feeling pure. For example, the things that help me function at the purest form of myself are going to church, praying, meditating, dancing, and practicing yoga. When I take care of myself, I can function as the purest form of myself, nourishing my experience to the best of my ability.

b. Santosha—contentment.

Being in a state of contentment is a quality we all possess, but not many of us practice it. We are a society that seeks. Being in a constant state of seeking means we will never be content. Instead, choose to be content. Still create a list of your desires, but move away from seeking. Be clear on what you want, simmer in the field of contentment, and watch the magic unfold.

c. Tapas—discipline.

What I love about being Mormon is that we are very disciplined in how we conduct ourselves and how we contribute to the world. I lived many years without this discipline. I easily settled for temporary pleasures, gave up too easily, and didn't feel worthy of much. While coming to know my heavenly Father's love for me, I learned that it would take work to become disciplined so that I could receive his blessings. Having this understanding has changed my life. I no longer struggle with life events I can't control or waste my life energy on things that don't serve me.

d. Svadhyaya—study of the sacred scriptures and of one's self.

I must admit that it took me a while after making the intention to commit to scripture study, because I did not know the blessings that came from it. When I finally engaged in it, my thoughts became clearer and more nourishing, I came to understand our heavenly Father more, and I came to better appreciate the love he has for us. Most of the answers to my prayers came through reading my scriptures or listening to conference talks from Mormonchannel.org.

e. Ishwara-pranidhana—surrender to the divine.

I have learned the hard way that we can't do everything on our own. We are not asked to. In Matthew 11:28, Jesus says, "Come to me all you who are weary and burdened and I will give you rest." Please know that you don't have to hold the heartaches, regrets, or anger. Surrender them to your heavenly Father, and do the work that you were sent here to do.

3. Asana—seat.

    Become aware of the flow of energy moving through your body through the art of yoga. I continue to evolve my self-practice in yoga because it makes me feel young and limber.

4. Pranayama—life force.

    Pranayama is the energy of breath moving through you. Breath is very powerful. There are many types of breaths you can embrace— breaths to invigorate the body or breaths to relax the body.

5. Pratyahara—withdrawing from the senses of the world to listen to the inner voice more clearly.

    Your inner voice will never compete with the distraction of the world or with the ego. Give yourself time to separate from these distractions to connect more deeply with the conscious being who resides within you.

6. Dharana—mastery of attention and intention.
   Where you place your life energy is where you
   will enhance in your life. Dr. Deepak Chopra
   said "attention energizes and intention
   transforms". Be careful of where you place
   your life energy, whether it's a thought,
   image, or experience. What you choose to
   focus on, you give it existence in this world.

7. Dhyana—development of the conscious being.
   Come to know the conscious being residing
   within you—the internal companion who
   has been with you since the first day of your
   existence, that still small voice within you.

8. Samadhi—oneness with all that exists.
   Samadhi gives us the understanding that we
   are all one and that we all come from the
   same source. Whatever you believe in, nature
   or a higher power, we are all a reflection
   of ourselves in different life experiences.
   Meaning at one time or another we have all
   felt sadness, lost, regret and alone. We are
   the same and desire the same things; peace,
   love, laughter, joy, acceptance and success.

The only differences between us are the ones you choose to believe.

Words of Wisdom

According to the law of the Words of Wisdom in Doctrine and Convents Section 89, 1-9, we are encouraged to not consume wine, strong drinks, tobacco, and hot drinks. In Ayurvedic medicine, which goes hand in hand with the yogic lifestyle, we are also encouraged not to partake in anything that would disrupt the natural cycles in the body. For example, the properties of caffeine increase the heart rate, giving us a temporary perception of "an energetic rush." The reality of drinking a caffeinated beverage is that a disruptor is increasing the body's heart rate and revving up all the body's systems.

Once I began to incorporate these teachings into my life, I found a great number of similarities between the Ten Commandments, the eight limbs of yoga, Words of Wisdom, and Ayurvedic medicine. Both lifestyles have provided me a great wealth of guidance in how to behave with integrity, love, and compassion. In today's culture, it is easy to gossip, judge, or be promiscuous. Reflect on your example and contribution. Whatever you permit in your environment, you promote. Be conscious of each choice you make. If you are having a difficult time deciding, ask yourself, "Is this choice nourishing me and those around me? Is this choice aiding in my evolution or encouraging stagnation in my life"?

I have found the yin and yang in life. I can testify that being Mormon has enhanced my understanding of my purpose and value, and yoga is a tool that expands my diversity to love all things, to be compassionate, and joyfully. I'm no longer afraid of the impermanence of life. My faith has taught me that we are here to learn and share and that we will all return home one day. With that said, let's make each day count as we continue to do heavenly Father's work and find one another in acts of love and service.

Embrace this moment as though it is the last moment in this time and place, because it truly is. Everything in life is impermanent. You will never experience this moment again. It's not promised that the people, opportunities, or relationships currently in your life will remain. Although the impermanence in life may cause pain, struggle, and sorrow, the true tragedy is when people linger over what they perceive to be lost. Experiences too are temporary, and we should flow through them. If we choose to linger, we choose to remain in the quicksand of painful thoughts. The longer you stay, the deeper the painful emotions will be felt and the longer it will take you to get out.

Observe nature. For instance, whether you are standing by the ocean, lying in a bed of grass, or standing in the middle of a forest, be aware. Nature expresses energetic life, radiating peace and harmony despite the turbulence that comes through its environment. Nature continues to manifest and evolve because that's its innate way of being. Interestingly, our innate way of being also is to evolve and manifest despite what turbulence comes through our environments. We can do so gracefully, radiating peace and harmony.

Dr. Wayne Dyer often spoke about the simplicity and complexity of life's processes. While developing in a mother's womb, a baby does nothing, yet the baby receives all he or she needs to sustain existence. After being born, the baby is introduced to his or her environment, where he or she continues to undergo transformations to adapt. A baby is influenced heavily by his or her environment. The child may be taught that he or she must work hard to get his or her needs met. And if the child's needs are not met, the child may be taught to feel shame and unloved. The child may be taught that physical possessions are required to palliate feeling shamed and unloved. The child may continue to work hard, fail, accumulate, and continue this vicious cycle. Sound familiar?

You carry the strength of nature and the genetic material from your ancestors within your body because your physical body consists of the recycled elements of this world. Your mind is made of the recycled thoughts and behaviors of your ancestors. The conditional mind is formed from all recycled information.

To strengthen or establish the connection with your inner essence, embrace a meditation practice. The body's stillness will allow the emotional mind to digest and process experiences, ultimately expanding the space between each thought. That in turn creates space between the stimulation of an experience to the way we choose to respond. When we don't allow time to digest, we create stagnation and find ourselves in the present moment thinking of the past or anticipating the future. This robs us from the gifts of the present moment. The present moment is when opportunities surface for us and when people we have yet to come to know are placed along our paths. If we are too distracted by the past and the future, we will miss the opportunities and encounters that will lead us to the manifestations of our deepest desires. Be still and process, allowing yourself to proceed into your journey with full intention and purpose. When you are so empowered to choose, you'll begin to stand firmly in your purpose and in the experience. Yes, in every experience you have a purpose. Observe it, connect with it, and own it.

My clients often ask me, "How can I get rid of negative thoughts?" or "How do I stop reliving the trauma or grief I've experienced?" First, express kindness to yourself. Trust that everything you have experienced has crossed your path to enhance your strength, faith, and wisdom. Find the opportunity and value in each experience. When you do, you will be set free from the struggle of trying to dissect the experience.

Keep in mind that meditation enhances awareness, reminding us that we are more than any temporary life experience. We don't use meditation to bypass the obstacles of life events. We are supposed to feel the pain, discomfort, rejection, and betrayal in order to be where we need to be and to help those we were sent here to help.

There is also another reason we may stagnate in experiences: we try to avoid them or we reject experiences completely unfolding because we don't want to feel the pain. However, the process of acceptance can release us from stagnating in the toxic emotions triggered by life's events. Acceptance is part of the law of karma. Each encounter and experience provides an opportunity for karma to run its course. When we learn from an experience, karmic energy has run its course. If we struggle with an experience, we interfere with the karmic energy; it will continue to repeat itself until it completely runs its course.

Instead of embracing struggle, look within and choose the most nourishing response to the karmic action that is unfolding. Some may need to brace themselves, but know that each karmic event is temporary. Responding in the most nourishing way is your responsibility and contribution to the experience. What has grounded me is the expression of "holding on to the iron rod" and prayer. Knowing that the end is in sight and that I should continue to hold on with a heart full of good intention and perseverance assures me that I will meet the divine loving energy of wisdom and strength at the end of the event.

In summary, own the art within *you*. You, my dear, are creative, unique, talented, kind, and courageous. Step away from your experiences and the things you have accumulated in your life, because you are more than these experiences. Your soul goes beyond what the mind is able to collect and translate. If you want to accomplish something, do it. Be unstoppable, or not. The choice is always yours.

There are three ways to embody the art of *you*.

1. *Pause* and embrace a meditation practice in which you allow thoughts, images, and sensations to surface. Be kind to yourself as you allow your mind to digest the experiences that surface. Even the undesirable thought may surface, for it too must be reevaluated or released through your consciousness.

2. *Shift* into a place where you can cultivate your intentions. When you have a destination or goal, it may become your main focus. Be careful, for you don't want to become too rigidly attached

to this destination or goal. As you evolve, your interest may change, or life events may interfere. Trust that there is a science that we may not understand immediately behind every outcome, but in its own way, this science is perfection at its best, enhancing strength, courage, and wisdom.

3. *Refresh* into the present moment with an awareness of purposeful choices and actions. Embrace the opportunities that surface, explore the unknown, and step out of your comfort zone.

Lead with the purest form of yourself, accept all for how it continues to unfold, and embrace your unique talents and abilities. In this way, you will establish the art of *you*.

Meditation Exercise for the Art of *You*

In our meditation exercise, I will introduce you to a mantra. A mantra is an instrument of the mind that helps you expand the space between your thoughts. Repeat your mantra five times before continuing to the next chapter.

Mantra: I lead my journey with the purest form of myself. How does that feel?

The Art of Intemperance

"The secret of Happiness ... is not found in seeking more, but in developing the capacity to enjoy less."

—Socrates

The art of intemperance teaches us that we live in an environment where it's easy to live beyond our means. Most of us lack moderation or restraint to eliminate the excess. In fact, most us own items that we don't utilize. I'll never forget a statement Dr. Wayne Dyer made. He said, "Most people only use 20 percent of what is in their closets." Does this statement apply to you? It sure did for me. I meditated on my own perceived wants and needs. My inner being encouraged me to evaluate and shift.

I owned a three-story house full of stuff that I thought I needed. Less than a year after my meditation on reevaluating my perceived wants and needs, I moved to a three-bedroom single home. I was amazed by how liberated I felt by giving things away. There was a different energy moving through my home. Shopping also changed for me. I became increasingly aware of the items I would purchase. I gave careful thought to how I would utilize the item, an approximation of how long it would be under my possession, and how I would dispose of it. I also considered who or what organization and purpose I would be supporting if I did purchase a certain item.

While completing my undergraduate degree in health science at Arizona State University, I enrolled in classes that opened my eyes to my carbon footprint and how I could lessen my impact on the world. I was appalled after reading statistics on carbon emissions, food waste, and where our trash was going. I couldn't believe that farmers and grocery store workers had to throw away edible produce because it was "misshapen" or that our government was having to buy land in third world countries in order to accommodate trash from the United States. We Americans use so much, yet we utilize so little.

Regarding food waste, a friend of mine who attended the same university was encouraged to be homeless for a class project. During this journey, he went scavenging for food at restaurants and grocery stores, looking through their dumpsters. He was surprised at the amount of food being thrown away. Most dumpsters were locked with a bar. However, he did come to a dumpster without a lock; he found enough food there to last him a week. I remember him visiting me with a bag of produce. At this point I didn't realize where he had retrieved the produce from. We made vegan banana ice cream and potatoes with avocado.

As I began to do my own research, I became overwhelmed and had to take a break. I then realized my soul was seeking time to reflect on the information I had come across and to explore my conditional mind. I was raised by a single mother who didn't have a high school education. She struggled to get by for many years. This taught me to be creative and to do more with less. However, what I saw on the television was a lifestyle that I felt the need to pursue in order to be happy. The life I was living didn't match what I was seeing. Although I felt content, the media convinced me that I would be happier with a big house, a fancy car, nice clothes, and world travels.

For many years, I was very much the unaware consumer. Maintaining this unaware consumer lifestyle was costly. I was living paycheck to paycheck. I thank all that is holy that I didn't come across some unforeseen tragedy or emergency. I don't know how I could have responded, having no savings. While living this unaware lifestyle, life became dull. I was filling the dullness with stuff, hoping it would bring back the spark of life. It did not. If anything, I found myself further in the dullness, becoming suffocated with stuff, and losing my grip on my finances.

Unfortunately, this lifestyle began to affect my intimate relationships. There was no love, compassion, passion, or playfulness. As my life spiraled, I began to make my family my only priority.

Then the dark cloud became darker. I lost someone I loved to addiction. I don't blame the media, the stuff, or being a consumer, but I do take responsibility for the lack of awareness I had during these times. I committed to living each day with full awareness of my choices. However, I am aware that people make their own choices and must suffer their own consequences.

In yoga, I teach that if we have strong connections with our bodies, minds, and souls, then making nourishing choices becomes easier. Listen to your body, for it is the compass navigating you to make the best choices possible. In the moment of struggle, connect within. Know that you can make the most beneficial choice.

An exercise I enjoy practicing is packing my lunch and making the commitment to not shop for anything. It's an amazing feeling to get home at the end of the day and know that I didn't spend a dime on anything. I valued my commitment as well as the environment.

There are three ways to explore the art of intemperance.

1. *Pause* and separate yourself from your experience for a moment. Witness yourself solely as the observer of your experiences, roles, possessions, thoughts, and conditional behaviors. Evaluate your needs, and explore your wants.

2. *Shift* to a state of nothingness in order to eliminate the excess. Create a space where no

intentional energy is being expended. Notice what surfaces. When you can come into this state of nothingness and be full of content in the presence of your own silence, then you will learn that you are enough and that no amount of stuff will ever fulfill you. My grandfather once told me, "Live like you're poor, and you'll be the richest person alive."

3. *Refresh* into a state of gratitude. Notice the things in your life you can be grateful for. For example, be grateful for your wellbeing at any condition or age. You have an energetic body, peaceful mind, and a compassionate heart.

Meditation Exercise for the Art of Intemperance

Repeat your mantra five times before continuing to the next chapter.

Mantra: I am grateful and content for who I am and all that I have.

How does that feel?

3 The Art of Ambiguity

"*I wanted a perfect ending. Now I've learned the hard way, that some poems don't rhyme, and some stories don't have a clear beginning, middle and end. Life is about not knowing, having to change, taking the moment and making the best of it without knowing what's going to happen next. Delicious Ambiguity.*"

—Gilda Radner

The foundation of ambiguity is uncertainty. Once we embrace uncertainty, we will understand the art of ambiguity. Embracing uncertainty can be uncomfortable. In this chapter, we will explore how to dive into uncertainty and embrace the beauty of the art of ambiguity, for it is a critical component of our wellbeing.

Let's take the physical body, for instance. There is a process in biology called adaptation by which the species that can physically and emotionally adapt to their environments are more likely to survive and evolve on their journeys. The species that cannot adapt will suffer and/or will die.

During a workshop with Dr. Deepak Chopra, he said, "If we only practice what we know then we are only repeating the past." Therefore, if we want different results, we must learn to respond differently to our experiences. Notice I said *respond*. Did you know that most *react* to their experiences instead of *responding* with intention and purpose?

What is the difference between reacting and responding? When we react there is very little time or space between the stimulus of the experience and when or where we contribute to that experience. When we respond, we create time and space between the stimulus of the experience and the response. This ensures that we will choose the best response that will nourish the experience. Being able to create time and space between stimulus and response requires much practice. The way we can enhance and expand this process is through meditation.

The type of meditation that has resonated with me is primordial sound mediation. In fact, I tried to meditate for many years until I met David Ji at the Chopra Center. It was there he told me to stop trying and just *be*. I was given my very own primordial sound mantra and began to incorporate it into in my beginning practices of just being. Primordial sound meditation changed my life. David Ji's kindness and simplicity changed my life. I would highly recommend his book, *Secrets of Meditation*. This is a great book for those who want to learn about meditation or for those who are establishing their practice.

As I observe and listen to conversations, I notice one common denominator: resistance to change. Furthermore, complaining and judging heavily influence most conversations, which is consistent to study conducted by researchers from the Netherlands and published December 8, 2012 in a CBS Cleveland article. These researchers stated that 90 percent of conversations are gossip.

Let's dissect the notion of complaining. Complaining means dissatisfaction with an experience, an outcome, or a response. Hey! Be kind to yourself. We have all been there! We can choose to live in this state of dissatisfaction, or we can choose a more desirable state. In order to know what is more desirable, one must know what to desire. What do you desire at the moment?

Once you find what you desire, then when you have a toxic thought you can shift into a more desirable time or space before you verbally express it into your external body, which is your environment. We have an obligation as infinite choice makers to contribute great things into our external bodies. When we choose to live in a toxic state, the toxicity will seep into our external bodies, inevitably contaminating everything in our bodies' paths.

Throughout my journey and my resistance to change, I have learned that clarity is a byproduct of ambiguity. The ambiguity of life scared me as a child. I moved around often after my parents' divorce. All I wanted was a home I could grow up in. I envied friends who were raised in the same house for their entire childhood.

Meanwhile, I moved twice in elementary school, four times in junior high, and three times in high school. I didn't move because my parents were in the military, but because they were trying to manage their own lives while raising three children. I've learned that when I resisted change, I caused myself additional pain. This self-inflicted pain was, at times, worse than the actual life event.

When I come across the word *ambiguity*, I think back to my childhood, when I first watched *Beauty in the Beast*, my favorite Disney movie. *Beauty and the Beast* is about a girl named Belle who is dissatisfied with life in her small town. Belle is fascinated with storybooks and is easily inspired by plots that expand her imagination. She knows there is more to life than the life she is living and desires to explore beyond what she knows.

In the midst of helping her father, who runs into trouble when he accidently trespasses, Belle nobly takes her father's punishment of imprisonment so her father can have his freedom. The man who arranges for the imprisonment is known as the Beast. The Beast was once cursed by an enchantress who saw no love in his arrogance. After time and effort, the Beast and Belle begin to fall in love, which breaks the Beast's curse. They then appear to live happily ever after.

In the beginning, Belle can't fathom all the possible

outcomes of her experience with the Beast. Belle leads with her heart through fear and uncertainty, with the understanding that if she is kind and loving, all will be well. Through my own journey, I approached life events with this same philosophy, which was instilled in me by my grandmother. During my parents' violent separation, moving multiple times, and watching my parents struggle with addiction, I knew that if I led each experience with kindness and love, I would be where I needed to be.

Every experience is temporary. Life events are not meant to stagnate, yet we tend to keep the memory of the struggle alive. The question is, are you allowing your experiences to repeat themselves in your mind or in your life? True suffering is not the experience. It's the choice of reliving the experience. Only you, my dear, can embrace the experience for what it is, extracting the value. Continuing to relive it causes self-inflicted suffering.

Notice that above I said, "your mind." Many clients of mine have been consumed by the way they have reacted to their experiences, feeling righteous or overwhelmed with guilt, anger, or sadness. Then they choose to stay in a space of perceived misery because their minds have settled into a stagnated state of hopelessness. In this state, it can be hard to see the reality of the present moment. The reason for this hopelessness is because they have drifted so deeply into their experiences that they have forgotten that they are the observers of those experiences and not the victims of them. Notice that when you are deep in a thought about the past you are no longer connected with what is happening in your present moment. You become disengaged or unfocused. This process wastefully expends energy, and you may become fatigued easily.

Let's do an exercise together that I have used often to shift from the slippery slope of stagnation to finding peace in the present moment. Take deep breaths, filling the lungs completely and allowing every inhalation to become deeper. After every inhalation, exhale through the mouth.

Now, shift into your fire-point energy breath. Take a couple of minutes here as you place the tip of your tongue to the roof of your mouth, breathing in and out of your nose. As you settle here in this time and space, what are the first thoughts that begin to surface?

Notice the thoughts. Know that they have surfaced for a reason. Maybe you can find their value. If you cannot find their value, then find the emotion attached to the experience. Once you can identify the emotion, then you can know what is feeding this thought. Take a deep breath and know that all is well and that you can release that thought. Allow yourself to create room for new experiences, new opportunities, and new love for yourself.

When you have an undesirable experience, move away from the quick reaction of complaining. Instead respond by rejoicing in the energy that has shaken your foundation. Find the beauty in the turbulence, for it has surfaced for a reason. You are the creator of your own peace.

Here are three ways to explore the art of ambiguity:

1. *Pause* and pray. Praying has been a big part of my daily practice. It helps me surrender and give my worries to the Lord. If we choose to carry our burdens alone, then we will find ourselves in a state of chaos. By nature, we are worshipers. If we don't believe in a higher force, then we will worship things that may not nourish our lives and each other.

2. *Shift* into the sensations of trust. Trust that at this moment, even if you feel uncertain, all is well because everything is as it should be.

3. *Refresh* into a profound feeling of acceptance. When you can accept all that has unfolded, then the impossible may just become possible. There is no room for stagnation when you accept everything that comes your way with the understanding that you cannot hold on to it. You must allow it to flow through you and away from you.

Meditation Exercise for the Art of Ambiguity

Repeat your mantra five times before continuing to the next chapter.

Mantra: All is well, because everything is as it should be.

How does that feel?

The Art of Surrendering

> *"Every time you are tempted to react in the same old way, ask if you want to be a prisoner of the past or a pioneer of the future."*

—Dr. Deepak Chopra

Do you ever find yourself in a moment when nothing is going according to plan? Perhaps this happens to us all more often than we'd like to admit. What if I told you that your plan is unreliable and an illusion that will limit you if you are rigidly attached to it? How would you respond? With anger? With curiosity? Our plans are based on what we know. When we can go beyond what we know, we will become who we are meant to be.

The mind cannot fathom the opportunities that

await us or the people we have yet to know. The best thing we can do is surrender in the present moment and embrace all that is surfacing with intention. Surrendering doesn't mean you do away with your responsibilities. It means you allow experiences to unfold naturally as you shift into a place of understanding. When the experiences are no longer nourishing you, the experiences have become an invitation to reevaluate. Don't waste your life energy resisting the moment by complaining or being angry. Shift away from complaining and being angry as you shift into understanding that all is as it should be as long as you are expressing your higher self.

Exploring the art of *you* will help expand your understanding of what it means to function at your highest self.

Your faith and values play vital roles in the art of surrendering. What activities are you engaged in that strengthen your faith and values? The best way to reflect on the answer to this question is to write down and meditate on the many activities you have engaged in during the last twenty-four hours. Where did you place your precious life energy?

By reflecting on the past twenty-four hours, we

may at times become aware of certain activities or reactions that we don't desire to repeat. This discovered awareness is a beautiful gift, encouraging you to pause, shift, and refresh, allowing you to live the life you desire. Embrace the activities that strengthen your faith and values. The stronger your faith and value system, the less you will be swept away by the strong current of temptation or life events.

Be mindful, and use your body to navigate every moment, for in every moment you will be surrounded by many options. There are a few options that will lead you closer to the manifestations of your desires. A good portion of my growth stems from the art of surrendering, which was not easy for me at first. I was introduced to the art of surrendering many times in my life but never considered it an art form until my grandmother passed away. That day was like no other; I was on my first flight to Hawaii. When I landed, I received the long-dreaded call. Never did I imagine that a moment I had longed for and a moment I had dreaded would collide the way they did.

I was in shock, pain, and disbelief. With the life I've come to know, shifting into a state of peace and gratitude can be easy. But that wasn't the case that day. Losing my grandmother took me to a whole other depth of pain that I had never experienced. Then I was confronted by my own understanding of the present moment.

In the present moment, we have the opportunity and the responsibility to respond with intention and purpose despite the pain being experienced and to move away from reacting impulsively. I caught myself reacting to the present moment with tears, regrets, loneliness, and fear. Acting out regrets, loneliness, and fear is not who I am nor what my grandmother deserves as she transitions. So, I did what I have been practicing for many years: I shifted to a space of peace and gratitude for the memories. It took more effort than I could even imagine, but I did it. I am truly blessed to have known my grandmother for thirty years and to have been influenced by her compassion, love, and generosity.

I've heard the expression "When it rains, it pours" many times in my life. Just as in nature, our tough experiences can seem to pour as soon as they begin to rain. We can be hit by one undesirable experience after the other. Unfortunately, we cannot expect people to understand or finish our work. Everyone is on his or her own journey. Be kind. If you reach out for help and there is no one there, be patient and don't give up. Do your work in the rain, and pray and trust that your heavenly Father will send help in his divine time.

During this time of loss, I received some e-mails about business that I had left unfinished prior to leaving. I became distracted by a friend's bike accident that sent him to the ICU a week prior to the trip. I spent a couple of days with him in the hospital.

I began to realize that I was continuing to help those who weren't willing to help themselves, and in the end my responsibilities and sanity were being compromised.

I was also in a relationship that felt one-sided. I had fallen in love, but there was so much uncertainty in the relationship that I was afraid I was wasting my time. How was it that all of this energy was accumulating?

I had to surrender to the fact that I cannot continue to try to fix the things that are not my doing. You see, when you jump into a situation to try to fix the outcome or "fluff" the landing for someone else's consequence, you will absorb the karma because you have chosen to contribute to their karmic episode.

What is a karmic episode? A karmic episode is an

experience, an event, or an encounter. Every karmic episode surfaces for a reason. Its purpose is to enhance the individual's courage, strength, and wisdom.

Allow events to unfold as they do. If the experience is not requiring your skill set, talent, or time, then continue to work on you; the experiences meant for you will surface. It is not your responsibility to help someone out of their experience. It is your responsibility to be mindful of how you are contributing to your own experience. Inspire those around you by leading with your spirit full of kindness, love, and compassion.

Life events will circle through despite our efforts to reduce turbulence. Life events are part of the constant field that will continue to flow into each and every one of our journeys. You can choose to resist life events or ride the wave. If you do choose the path of resistance, then you are embracing self-inflicted suffering; this may continue to happen until you become aware of the conscious choice maker within. Be kind to yourself during this process.

I've watched my own family and those around me blame others for how life events unfolded. Why do we do this? Here is my observation: we have become too busy—so busy, in fact, that we have become unaware of our own actions, contributions, and words. Another observation is that a sense of comfort begins to set in, and we no longer evolve. When we are comfortable, there is no need to change or evaluate our experiences.

Notice that it's not so much the life event that causes suffering. It's how we respond. There is nothing we can do about this circulation of life events other than live life with full attention and awareness of how we are contributing to the life event with our time and energy. If we live life by paying attention with intention and purpose, then these events will pass. When you flow with the experience, you may even find the value and purpose of a given life event. If we live life based on the conditional mind and impulsively react, then we may have more turbulence in our lives. Naturally, we need some turbulence to enhance our courage, strength, and perseverance. However, it can be easy to expend unnecessary life energy on unnecessary activities that feed into unnecessary turbulence.

Once I shifted my thoughts to the present moment, I began to settle into a state of gratitude and noticed the synchronicities that were surfacing.

One synchronized event was that I had purchased the Hawaii trip a year prior because Dr. Wayne Dyer was going to be a guest speaker at the "Seduction of Spirit" retreat at the Chopra event in Maui, Hawaii. However, Dyer passed away about five months after I had purchased the trip. I no longer had the desire to go. However, after some deep reflection, I took Dyer's passing as a gift, because I would have never purchased the tickets to Hawaii if he hadn't been going. Now that my money was nonrefundable, something was calling me to Maui—something bigger than I could comprehend. Being with my Chopra family was therapeutic for me during the time of my grandmother's passing.

Another synchronized experience that happened while I was in Hawaii still brings tears to my eyes. Before receiving the call about my grandmother, I was scrolling through Facebook when I stopped at a spiritual gangster advertisement. Spiritual gangster sells trendy yoga clothing. The advertisement was a photograph of a woman wearing a sweater that said, "Here Comes The Sun." I paused with a smile, because it reminded me of one of my favorite songs by the Beatles. Even just the song's intro brings a smile to my face. Then the call came.

We went through the motions to get to the hotel; our second flight was delayed. Anytime I felt the emotions that came along with being a victim of circumstance, I would think back to how I felt when I read, "Here Comes The Sun" Then it became easier to shift into peace and gratitude.

I arrived at the Ritz Carlton about five hours later than expected. But it was the perfect time, because as I entered, I heard someone playing the ukulele, and guess what song the musician was playing? That's right. "Here Comes the Sun." A few days into the "Seduction of Spirit" retreat, we had a ceremony to honor Dr. Wayne Dyer's life and those who have passed. We all stood out on the lawn at the Ritz Carlton, overlooking the water. It was stunning. We had the most beautiful meditation, and afterwards we danced in celebration of all our loved ones who had passed. The last song played was "Here Comes the Sun." How could this be? I cried and hugged those around me. I looked out to the water and up at the sky and said, "Thank you. I love you."

Everything in life is impermanent. Release what no longer is serving you and find the blessing of how life is unfolding before your eyes! The reason why letting go is vital to our evolution is because life experience are not meant to be held on to, regardless of how lovely or horrible they were or how tightly you hold on to them. You are only causing yourself more suffering when you hold on to people, things, or experiences.

There are three ways to practice the art of surrendering:

1. *Pause*: Release what no longer has a place in your life. You are an infinite creator and can choose to live a life you desire. In order to release, you must pause. This pause is where you give yourself the opportunity to allow information to surface through your consciousness. In this release, you have the opportunity to find the wisdom, courage, and strength needed to recognize the information that has been disguised in your physical body.

2. *Shift* into the confidence that every experience has the purpose of enhancing your courage, strength, and wisdom. In this realm of confidence, you liberate yourself from trying to control things that occur. Occurrences don't surface by your control, so they are not meant to be controlled. As soon as you begin to

manipulate the information in your body based on the limited mind, you will meet resistance and stunt your evolution. Trust and just be as you embrace the information that is surfacing just for you.

3. *Refresh*: Embrace the moment for how it is unfolding.

Meditation Exercise for the Art of Surrendering

Repeat your mantra five times before continuing to the next chapter.

Mantra: I surrender to the flow of life.

How does that feel?

5 The Art of Conscious Choices

"Authenticity is not something we have or don't have. It's a practice—a conscious choice of how we want to live. Authenticity is a collection of choices that we have to make every day. It's about the choice to show up and be real. The choice to be honest. The choice to let our true selves be seen."

—Brene Brown

Take a moment here. Reflect on the blessings of being a human being. You are a part of the smartest and most talented species known to exist. Not only do you hold the capacity of manifesting creative inventions, but you are also alive in a time when anything you desire can be yours with minimal work due to evolution and the convenience of the modern world.

Using one hand, you can market, connect, and research. It is amazing how far technology is evolving. Children are learning more things earlier. The wealth of accessible information is immense. How can you navigate through all of this information? How can you excel in your own creative way? On a deeper level, who's leading your journey at this moment? Think about it: How many choices have you made that were led by the spirit and full of intention and purpose? Or how many choices have you made with the mind?

For many years, my choices felt automatic. I was unaware of the significance and the power of my desires. My choices where the results of my circumstances. I was allowing results to just happen without any intention or desire to navigate what was manifesting in my life.

After becoming a yoga instructor, I quickly began to realize that most of my emotions and choices were automatic reactions to my experiences based on my past circumstances and those who have influenced me in some way. I had become a victim of my own circumstances. With this profound realization, I was empowered to live my life full of intention. Ultimately,

I was moving away from reacting and moving toward responding in the most nourishing way.

Making conscious choices is a pivotal part of living an intentional life. I started by first changing my thoughts. I was no longer going to waste time and my life energy on thoughts or illusions that were fueling my fear, insecurity, and doubt. Thoughts can rob us from the gifts of the present moment. When you are distracted by a thought, you lose awareness of your present moment.

The Three Realms of Thoughts

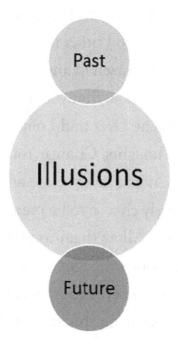

When thoughts from the past seep into the present moment it may fog our clarity to see the reality unfolding before our eyes. This fog is the accumulation of residue from past experiences. Your future thoughts are anticipations of assumptions based on your past experiences and the experiences you have witnessed. Illusions can be formed when the realms of the past and future are being experienced. These illusions take us further away from the present moment. At times, we can begin to believe the illusions we are creating. "I'm going to lose my job." "He doesn't think I'm attractive anymore." "I am never going to stop smoking." "I will never get married." "My biological clock is ticking." "I'm too old." "The good times have passed."

When you find yourself in any of these realms, take a deep breath and know that you are more than your thoughts. As Wayne Dyer and Louise Hay have said, "Change Your Thoughts, Change Your Life."

Dr. Deepak Chopra says you are an infinite choice maker. Consciously choose to be present, for thoughts will come and go. Allow them to move through you. If you fantasize about a thought too long, you will shift further away from the present moment.

Be kind to yourself, for this art of making conscious

choices is a practice. The more you become aware of practicing conscious choice making, the easier it will become to choose the right choice for yourself. Before you begin to make a choice, take time to first explore your thoughts, behaviors, and choices. To understand who you have become and how you are contributing to your experience is vital to your expansion.

A great exercise to enhance the focus and clarity of your conscious choices is to recapitulate the previous day.

Sit comfortably, gently close your eyes, and take a few cleansing breaths as you inhale through your nose and exhale through your mouth five times. Then shift into your fire point energy breath, as described earlier. As a reminder, place the tip of your tongue to the roof of your mouth. There is a little ridge behind your two front teeth. Place the tip of your tongue there as you continue to breathe in through your nose and exhale through the nose. Now begin to recapitulate your previous day from the moment you woke up. What were your first thoughts? Who was the first person that came to your mind? How did you nourish yourself? Who did you speak to? Were you kind to yourself and to others?

Give yourself time to sit in silence and recap.

Once you complete your exercise, write down some things that surfaced and reflect on them.

Even while being a conscious choice maker, it's easy to shift into an emotion and allow the emotion to navigate your response. Remember that you are more than the emotion that has been cultivated on this journey. When we allow our emotions to navigate the choices we make, then we can easily shift into self-inflicted suffering, whether we are conscious of it or not.

There are two different types of suffering. One is life events and the other is the choice to linger in the residue and thoughts of the life events. The deepest suffering comes from choosing to linger and relive the life event.

Life events are inevitable. Ride the wave of the events. The moment you try to resist the wave, you will suffer.

Hopefully, you now know how powerful your life energy is, wherever you place it. Whether it's a thought or a life event, you will give it power and space in your life.

1. *Pause:* Become aware of your choices through the exercise of recapitulation.

2. *Shift* into the power of your energetic being. Use your energy for endeavors that will encourage you to function at your purest self by making conscious choices.

3. *Refresh:* Stand firmly in the conscious power that you possess. I've learned to enhance my conscious power by meditating, practicing yoga, reading my scriptures, and becoming involved in community service.

Meditation Exercise for the Art of Conscious Choices

Repeat your mantra five times before continuing to the next chapter.

Mantra: I can consciously choose the best response. How does that feel?

The Art of Transitioning

"Life is like riding a bicycle. To keep your balance, you must keep moving."

—Albert Einstein

To understand the art of transitioning, we must first accept that we are in a constant state of transition. You don't have the same body you had ten years ago. You have a new set of liver cells, hair cells, and fingernails, and you have embraced new understandings.

With that said, every minute you are transitioning. Everything in this life is impermanent, meaning everything has a life cycle. Opportunities, relationships, and physical items will come and go.

The art of transitioning can be masked by loss,

separation, and death. The moment we experience loss, it's easy to drift into suffering, because we were attached to what we lost. Every drift is a choice; empower yourself to be intentional about what you drift towards. If you if catch yourself energizing a thought or illusion, stop yourself and say, "I honor this thought and release it with love and gratitude, but I choose to live in the present moment."

You have so much power over your thoughts. Don't become the victim of the mind that was created by thoughts of the past. Become the creator living in the present moment and creating the most amazing life that you desire.

I was once stuck in a thought, and the thought became my life. I was born into an abusive family and thought that love was full of suffering and pain. I was not enough. I carried this thought through my first long-term relationship, in which it was painful to love and receive love. Then came his first affair. I allowed it because I knew I would never be enough for him. It wasn't until his third affair when I came to know my own worth. Twenty-eight years later, I was learning what love was through the eyes of people who knew me—not my family, for they too were masked by suffering and could not see anything else. I saw my reflection through the eyes of my children, my patients, my clients, and my family ward. My "family ward" refers to my friends from church. These people knew my heart and loved me unconditionally. I didn't have to try to be anything. They loved me because they understood the love of our heavenly Father.

After my divorce, I was in the deepest state of pain. I was in my twenties, and I held my sobbing and confused children at night while they asked for their dad. I worried about paying the bills, as I was still completing my undergraduate degree and only making twelve dollars an hour. The only thing sustaining me was unconditional love, a force I had only felt when I lived with my grandmothers. I was grateful to have this love, for it was all that I had fueling me.

Working during the day and staying up at night to study was hard. Every other moment was spent doing my best to emotionally stabilize the kids and assure them that all would be okay while I was breaking with financial worry.

One day I heard a knock at the front door. I couldn't bear to answer it due to the pain I was experiencing from the divorce. For some weird reason, I had found comfort in the pain I had come to know. I didn't answer the door. Then a few days later, the same knock came. I felt a sense of comfort this time. Something was telling me that this door, if I chose to open it, would be the pathway to the life I had been praying for.

During this time, I filled my days with many silent moments and noticed that this still, small voice inside of me was becoming louder and guiding me away from the pain I once knew.

The person behind the door was the kindest woman I have met thus far, Stacy Smith. She is known to be my angel, my Santa Clause, and my best friend. Stacy introduced herself, gave me a candy apple, and invited me to church. When she left, she asked if there was anything she could do for me. All I could say was please pray for us.

A few weeks later, I started going to church. Meeting so many like-minded people was refreshing and provided me a sense of hope to evolve into the person I desired to be. I was finally provided the environment where I can love myself enough to start healing the wounds from the past that I had unconsciously and consciously held on to. Everything was falling into place. I was encouraged to release what I could no longer control and shift into all that I had, which was the energy of love.

To this day, my mission is to love, hug, and kiss all of those who come to me. All that I have drawn to me was because of this shift into unconditional love. Today, I am involved in many nonprofit projects that help victims of domestic violence, caregivers, stroke survivors, and those with low income build their confidence through yoga, meditation, and modern techniques. Allow love to fuel you, and watch your life change. If you are unaware of how to cultivate love in your life, you will find it through community service.

Another example of transitioning is death. When my grandmother passed away, I was full of pain. Her presence enriched my life. All that was left was her imprint on my soul.

When one event ends, another begins. As nature evolves, it doesn't complain or refuse to grow. It naturally flows, regardless of whatever turbulence comes through its environment, and it will continue to manifest and survive.

You too can manifest your desires and not just survive but thrive beyond life events. Embrace all that comes your way—especially turbulence, for turbulence is where you will learn the most. It's there to help you evolve into higher levels of strength, courage, and faith. Be strong, sweet soul. Be strong.

1. *Pause* and be still. The pace of life can be move faster than our blossoming awareness. If you are in limbo or experiencing turbulence, be still and take a breath. Feel the life force entering your being and exiting. Dr. Deepak Chopra once said, "In the moment of chaos, be still." In the Bible, Psalm 46:10 says, "Be still, and know that I am God."

2. *Shift* into the realm of possibilities. Trust the wisdom of a higher source to have a divine plan for you. That plan is beyond what you can comprehend. Once I dived into the mindset of all possibilities, I tapped into unlimited source of growth, trust, and comfort. Be still, and know that what you are experiencing has a greater meaning. There is no need to know why and how right now. Proceed to flow. The moment you resist or stagnate by demanding to know the why and how something has occurred, you will accumulate suffering.

3. *Refresh* by leading with love. When you wake up, lead with love. Invite all encounters. Make it a mission to love and meet one new person each day, and watch the love within you deepen and your social life begin to change. Just aim for one person each day, starting with you.

Meditation Exercise for the Art of Transitioning

Repeat your mantra five times before continuing to the next chapter.

Mantra: I trust the process of life.

How does that feel?

The Art of Self-Preservation

> "The preservation of peace and the guaranteeing of man's basic freedoms and rights require courage and eternal vigilance: courage to speak and act—and if necessary, to suffer and die—for truth and justice; eternal vigilance that the least transgression of international mortality shall not go undetected and unremedied."
>
> —Haile Selassie

The art of self-preservation came to me during the perceived lack of an unfulfilled desire. This profound awareness saved my second long-term relationship for a duration. I made the mistake in placing too much power on what I was expecting. Greed can easily be masked by the feelings of an unfulfilled desire. In this last art, you will learn how to preserve your life energy and fulfill your own desires. Shift your energy from what you perceive to lack to something you can create.

After many attempts to get my significant other's attention intimately, I failed. How was our intimacy diminishing only nine months in? Any time the mind shifted into failure, it began to blame, categorize, or find a solution.

My ego quickly shifted to ask the emotional conditional mind what was wrong with me. He no longer reached for me as much. This was new territory for me. I had never had to try so hard to get a man's attention.

I could have responded in two ways, based on my past experiences. I could have reacted conditionally by asking, *Who is receiving his intimate affection, if I'm not? Does he still desire me? Does he find me to be grotesque?* Because that's how I was beginning to feel every time he would push me away.

Or I could respond by reflecting on my desires. Which do you think I led with? Well I wanted to settle in comfort and react, since I was in an undesirable place. However, I chose to reflect. I awoke early and went to work. I gave myself time to meditate away from my traditional place. I was experiencing something new and knew that I had to find a different space to honor this new growth being offered to me.

While in my meditation, the words *self-preservation* came to me. Eureka! My relationship was not lacking intimacy. I had lost control of my desires. Complete control. The ego was content in this time of my life. Weekly, I was achieving most of my desires. I was on a high and wanted more. I was expecting more than what he was willing to give. Instead of wasting my life energy on what was lacking, I used that life energy to fulfill other desires.

It's easy to become so excited by the gifts of life that we become greedy, wanting more than what's being offered. Be aware that some people and the emotional state of mind that comes with unfulfilled desires may fuel a certain belief by telling you that you're not asking too much; you deserve it, or you can get it somewhere else. Life does not work that way. Nature does not work that way. If you become greedy, scarcity becomes visible. If you are grateful, contentment becomes visible.

In the book *Seven Spiritual Laws of Success* by Dr. *Deepak Chopra*, we are taught by the fourth law to be mindful of how we expend our life energy. It's easy to expend life energy everywhere. Life is exciting, and to be a part of everything possible is amazing—except the fact that not everything you invest your life energy in will enhance the quality of your life in the long run.

Be careful here. Expend your energy on endeavors that will enhance the quality of your life, such as family time, education, service, and self-care.

1. *Pause:* Take time to reflect on what you desire. Is it realistic? Is it nourishing for you and those around you?
2. *Shift* from greed to gratefulness. Through my life journey I've learned that I may not have always received what I wanted, but I have received what I've needed.
3. *Refresh* into enhancing your awareness of where you are placing your life energy. Where you place your life energy is what you will enhance. Be mindful of where you place your thoughts, actions, and talents.

Meditation Exercise for the Art of Self- Preservation

Repeat your mantra five times before continuing to the next chapter.

Mantra: I am mindful of how I expend my energy.

How does that feel?

Establishing Harmonious Oneness

"Twenty years from now you will be more disappointed by the things you didn't do than by the ones you did do. So throw off the bowlines. Sail away from the safe harbor. Catch the trade winds in your sails. Explore. Dream. Discover."

—Mark Twain

Before I dive into how I incorporated these seven arts into my life, I want to share a personal story with you that shook me to my core and really helped me catapult myself out of the conditional mind and into living a life full of awareness and intention.

During one of my shifts at a hospital, I was walking

down the hall when I saw this sobbing woman outside of a room. I couldn't help but ask her if there was anything I could do to help. She looked up at me and said, "If you really want to help me, you'll hear me out. My husband and I raised three boys and worked two jobs at a time so that when we reached retirement we could enjoy ourselves. We are not a year in retirement, and we just found out he has stage four pancreatic cancer and is only expected to live six months."

My heart was broken, and it was clear that she was not only in pain but angry. I was completely frozen. Usually I can be quick with condolences; working at the hospital means it's typical to hear these kinds of stories.

It appeared as though my lack of response calmed her. She looked at me and said, "If you really want to help, please don't wait to do the things you want to do; do them now. Live now, because tomorrow is not guaranteed." She walked away, and I probably stood there for another minute as tears began to surface.

This story took the cake, because her words pierced through my soul and paralyzed my body. It was almost as though I was meant not to respond but to take the role as a silent witness.

My perspective on life changed after that encounter. She was my angel. I began to count my blessings, began my spiritual mission, and held my family closer than ever.

Establishing harmonious oneness is subjective. Everyone has his or her own variation of what *harmony* means. By the term *establishing*, I don't mean that you are creating something that was never there. The field of harmony is within you. In the Oxford English Dictionary, *establishing* means to set up on a firm or permanent basis. You don't need to try to be harmonious. Just bring your awareness to the purest state of yourself, the state of gratitude, love, and contentment. You'll always have the choice between having a "mind shift" or simmering in "mind sh*t."

There is a misconception that the accumulation of physical possessions, relationships, and accomplishments can bring you harmony. If that's the case, then your harmony is temporary. What happens when you lose your physical possessions? Or when you have to leave a relationship? Or when you lose your reputation? If you rely on experiences to bring you harmony, then your harmony is temporary—for, as we learned in the last chapter, all experiences are impermanent.

The arts enhanced my awareness that harmony is within. Knowing this truth, I found freedom from control, contentment in my choices, and the ability to explore unconditional love. Coming to know the harmony within me made it easier to embrace acts of love, kind gestures, compassion toward diversity, and acceptance of all that is. All of this nourished the harmony within. It became a beautiful, dynamic exchange.

How would your world change if every day you committed to one act of love? Or what if every day you made one kind gesture? Became compassionate toward diversity? Accepted yourself and all that has occurred? This is your time to live the life you desire and be the person you wish to be.

What are some things you can do this week to establish harmonious oneness in your life?

Meditation Exercises

Ideally, try to meditate for thirty minutes twice a day. With my attention span, thirty minutes was way too long in the beginning, and every time I attempted to meditate, I felt as though I was failing. I knew there had to be another way to establish a meditation practice. I started out repeating a mantra five times in the morning, at lunch, and before bed. Then I found myself craving to sit in stillness for five minutes while repeating the mantra. I continued to work my way up. Now forty-five minutes seems to fly by.

I encourage you to choose the variation that is practical and convenient for you.

Quick Guide to Arts and Mantras

- **The Art of *You*:** I lead my journey with the purest form of myself.
- **The Art of Intemperance:** I am grateful and content for who I am and all that I have.
- **The Art of Ambiguity:** All is well, because everything is as it should be.
- **The Art of Surrendering:** I surrender to the flow of life.
- **The Art of Conscious Choices:** I can consciously choose the best response.
- **The Art of Transitioning:** I trust the process of life.
- **The Art of Self-Preservation:** I am mindful of how I expend my energy.

About the Author

Ericka Brian also known as Ericka Martinez was born in Los Angeles, California. She is a graduate of Arizona State University, Chopra Center University, and Health Science Academy. As founder of Return to Yourself Wellness LLC, Ericka can be found teaching yoga, meditation, and nutrition workshops around Arizona and online.

To reach her personally, e-mail her at Ericka@ returntoyourself.org, or to get a list of her services and events, go to www.returntoyourself.org.

Visit the Chopra Center!

There are many wonderful workshops that contributed to Ericka's journey. Go to www.chopra.com, reach out to a Chopra represented and mention Ericka Brian as your referral source. Some recommendations:

- ❖ Weekend Within
- ❖ Journey into healing
- ❖ Healing the heart
- ❖ Seduction of Spirit
- ❖ Silent awakenings

Pause   Shift   Refresh